Great Perennials

From Bud to Seed

Great Perennials

Photographs by Carol Sharp

Words by Clare Foster

From Bud to Seed

conran
OCTOPUS

First published in 2001 by Conran Octopus Limited
a part of Octopus Publishing Group
2–4 Heron Quays, London E14 4JP
www.conran-octopus.co.uk

Publishing Director Lorraine Dickey
Senior Editor Muna Reyal
Editor Galiena Hitchman

Creative Director Leslie Harrington
Executive Art Editor Megan Smith
Designer Caz Hildebrand

Production Director Zoe Fawcett
Production Controller Alex Wiltshire

British Library Cataloguing-in-Publication Data.
A catalogue record for this book is available from the British Library.

ISBN 1 84091 189 1

Colour origination by Sang Choy International, Singapore

Printed in China

Contents

Foreword by Carol Sharp

My garden is my sanctuary. It is also my studio and a canvas for my passion – plants. I have gradually filled it with plants that fascinate me in all their stages. I've noticed I am drawn continually over the year to those that have more than just a glorious flower; some plants have intriguing buds and seedheads and even interest in the foliage, which may often change colour over the seasons.

By continually photographing them in different lights and from different angles I have to look and look again, and still I see more. The closer I get the more is revealed, the lens unveiling much more than you can see with the naked eye. As I wander among them I watch their characters emerge – changing every day, as they perform their part in the great theatre of the garden. To do justice to the drama I see unfolding, I have decided to present them in four main scenes.

Scene One: Bud The bud has an exquisite secret which makes it all the more alluring. It is usually green but bursting with promise of the colour that is yet to come.

Scene Two: Bloom The flower is the peak of the performance: whether unassuming or exuberant, a flower always fills me with intense joy. The rich variation of shapes and colours never cease to amaze me. Looking closer the petals lead you to the centre and the intricate design of the stamens and stigma.

Scene Three: Foliage Although the leaves are first to appear, they play a supporting role and must wait until Scene Three to take centre stage. While lacking the drama of the bud or bloom, the leaves often have special interest and provide a sound structure for the main performers.

Scene Four: Seed The vehicle the plant has devised to disperse its seeds often appears to echo the flower in a very avant-garde way. This is often my favourite part of the performance.

No two years' performance will be the same, as the conditions vary from year to year, and although every year I anticipate each stage, it is still with a sense of wonder that I see the constant cycle of growth unfold, marking the passage of time in the garden.

A year in the garden

In the short, bitter days of January there's not a lot to photograph, so the emerging buds of the hellebore are all the more exciting. I have to lie on the ground to get low enough to look into the face of the beautiful nodding flowers in February. By March I spot the silvery feathery foliage of the Pasque flower, its bud encased in a silken skein haloed with the sun behind it. Its beautiful purple flowers appear, and I know that spring is here.

In April the fat bud of the peony opens for its glorious but brief flourish and I have to be sure I don't miss the shot. I circle the strange flower of the columbine and decide it is most dramatic in profile. I shoot the gorgeous, fluffy bronze fennel foliage against leaves behind, bright green in the May sun. By June the tiny spiky buds of the cardoon can be seen nestling in the now huge silver leaves, the days are long and warm and it is summer at last.

The sea holly flowers are like blue stars, shot from directly overhead in the July haze. The Pasque flower seedheads are like sparklers and the strands look like hairy spider's legs through my close-up lens. The delicate buds of the fennel unfurl in August into masses of yellow umbels. The plants are so tall I have to get my ladder to reach the buds. Below, the golden groundsel buds burst into sunny orange daisies and I try several angles to give the stamens some form.

By September our latecomers are in bud. The bobbles on the lengthening bugbane stalk finally froth into a mass of stamens, frocked by tiny petals. I go to Piet Oudolf's new garden in Norfolk to capture them *en masse*. While there I take more shots of the coneflower, also featured in his prairie-style planting in the garden. The sweep of rusty pink is very dramatic.

Back in my garden the peony seedheads have popped open exposing the shiny black seeds briefly before the rain washes them away. I shoot the foliage again now, glowing purple, red and green in the soft October light. The coneflower has dropped all its petals leaving the cone which will blacken during November. The sea holly still looks proud and I shoot it from the side to show the structure.

I shiver as I'm up early to catch the frost defining the fluffy seedhead of the golden groundsel and the tall skeletons of the fennel against the cold blue sky. It's December and the evergreen, glossy serrated leaves of the hellebore shelter the emerging buds to start the whole cycle again.

Introduction

Perennials – herbaceous plants that return with new growth each year – have been cultivated ever since gardens began, weaving in and out of fashion over the centuries. In the Renaissance period they were grown with bulbs, herbs and shrubs in knot gardens, while in the Landscape period of the eighteenth century they were relegated to the walled garden, out of sight of the main house. Later, in the late nineteenth century, the herbaceous border became popular as a reaction against the elaborate bedding schemes that had dominated the first half of that century, and soon even small gardens had borders stuffed full of perennials. After World War II, however, with labour scarce, many herbaceous borders were grassed over and it is only in the past decade that growing perennials has enjoyed a revival.

And when you think about it, why not? The role of perennials in the garden is invaluable, forming the backbone of the flower garden. Returning year after year, they offer different interest throughout the seasons, from the time when the first shoots push through the soil to the forming of the seedheads in autumn. Probably the most diverse plant group, there are hundreds of species to choose from and even more varieties (known as 'cultivars') that have been bred artificially by nurserymen, providing an enormous variety of shape, colour and texture, from low, ground-covering plants to tall, architectural specimens such as the magnificent cardoon. Most mature perennials need little maintenance apart from deadheading to prolong the blooms, and dividing every three to five years to improve vigour and increase stock. Many, like those chosen for this book, don't even need to be cut back in winter, their seedheads providing visual interest in the garden as everything else dies back around them. In short, the value of perennials can never be understated. There are perennials for everyone, and we hope this book will whet your appetite to explore their considerable potential.

A note on plant names

The nomenclature of plants can be confusing. Often, the Latin botanical name (genus plus species, for example *Cynara cardunculus*) is supplemented by a common name (in this instance 'cardoon') which can vary from country to country, even region to region. To complicate things further, if the plant is a cultivated version of the species (cultivar), it will have another name added after the genus and species, for example *Cimicifuga simplex* 'Brunette'. In this book, we have used the common name as far as possible, although if we are referring to a specific cultivar we have used the full Latin name plus cultivar.

Columbine

Aquilegia 'Crimson Star'

Bud

Poised to take off in mid spring, the bud of Aquilegia 'Crimson Star' is like a little red rocket. Its compact shape will soon unfurl to reveal the full glory of the flower.

With delicate, nodding flowerheads, columbines are capricious plants with a reputation for promiscuity – as anyone who has grown them will know, columbines cross-pollinate freely with the help of bees, creating new seedlings with curious variations. Growing wild throughout the northern hemisphere in damp meadows, woodland and mountains, most columbines have distinctive bell-shaped flowers with five elegant spurs projecting back like wings. This characteristic is reflected both in their botanical name (from the Latin *aquila*, eagle) and in the common name, which derives from the medieval Latin *columbina*, meaning belonging to a dove or pigeon.

'One of the stars of the season'
HELEN DILLON

There are many historical references, from a watercolour of *Aquilegia vulgaris* by the sixteenth-century artist Albrecht Dürer to listings in herbals that show the popularity, or otherwise, of the plant. William Robinson mentions 63 aquilegias in his 1904 edition of *The English Flower Garden*, and judged them as 'singularly beautiful'. Reginald Farrer, however, was scathing about the plant in his 1919 book *The English Rock Garden*: 'This race is correspondingly difficult and miffy in temper' and 'as short-lived as a mid-Victorian heroine'. Today, the columbine has no medicinal uses, but records show that the seed was used in the past in herbal remedies. In his *New Herball* (1568), the Reverend William Turner likened the columbine seeds to fleas, and noted that 'if drunk with wine it is good for jaundice'.

Aquilegia 'Crimson Star' is a fiery, spirited addition to an informal spring border or wildflower meadow, thriving in moist soil. Its flowers appear in late spring from orange-red buds on branched stems, and won't fade until midsummer. The sticky, lime-green seed pods mature to a papery brown: this is the time to collect and sow the tiny black seeds.

Bloom

The pretty flowers of 'Crimson Star' have five spurs behind the colourful petals, a trait common to most columbines. Measuring 3–7cm (1¼–2¾in) long, the flowers are held singly or in clusters on branched, leafy stems, and last from late spring to midsummer.

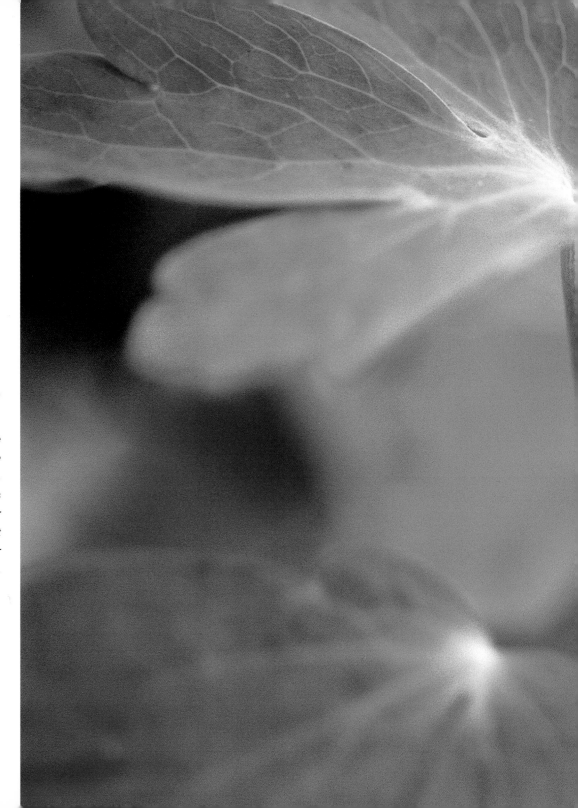

14

Foliage

Columbine leaves are pleasantly rounded, like large clover leaves, arranged in rosettes around the stems. Water droplets stand out beautifully on their smooth surfaces.

Height 60cm (24in)
Spread 30cm (12in)

Cultivation

Columbines enjoy moist soil, but it should not be waterlogged, so a dressing of grit to aid drainage is helpful. They grow best in dappled shade, but will tolerate full sun if given plenty of humus and grit. They are fully hardy.

Propagation

It is best to propagate columbines from seed, as division is difficult. Seed should be sown in containers in a cold frame as soon as ripe in late summer. Water the seedlings when they appear in spring, and by May they will be ready to transplant. All columbines self-seed profusely but also hybridize freely.

Pests and diseases

Columbines are susceptible to powdery mildew, aphids, leaf miners, sawflies and caterpillars.

Associations

Columbines look good in an informal setting with other 'cottage garden' plants such as foxgloves, hollyhocks and delphiniums.

Seed

As the petals disappear, the seedheads of the columbine develop, once again pointing upwards towards the sun. Like jesters' hats, the seedheads are at first a vivid lime green with a sticky surface, drying to a papery consistency as time goes on (see page 96). The black seeds look a little like mouse droppings.

Cardoon

Cynara cardunculus

An unashamed exhibitionist, the cardoon is the prima donna of the flower garden, performing with huge aplomb at the back of a border with its stunning silver-grey foliage and massive thistle-like flowerheads – perhaps the most architectural of all border perennials. Native to well-drained, sunny grassland in the Mediterranean, the cardoon is grown primarily as an ornamental plant, although in Italy and some parts of France it is used as a winter vegetable by blanching the lower leaves and stems in autumn. Low in calories and celery-like in appearance and taste, it can be steamed or chopped and eaten raw in salads. It should not be confused with its close relative, the globe artichoke (*Cynara scolymus*), whose buds are frequently eaten – delicious with melted butter or vinaigrette. In French potagers, cardoons are often grown in rows as hedges, while in the English flower garden these clump-forming giants provide strong accents in sunny borders, producing towering spikes of purple flowers in mid or late summer.

Both the cardoon and the artichoke have been cultivated since Greek and Roman times. Pliny referred to the cardoon as being prized above all other garden herbs, while Dioscorides used the mashed roots as a kind of deodorant. The artichoke has always been considered an aristocratic vegetable, and was favoured by Henry VIII, partly because he believed it to be an aphrodisiac. In recent years, the value of the globe artichoke as a medicinal herb has been discovered, to improve liver and gall bladder function and lower blood cholesterol. An old recipe from the Mediterranean region uses the juice from fresh artichoke leaves mixed with wine or water as a liver tonic, while in Portugal, dried cardoon flowerheads are used by traditional cheesemakers as a coagulent.

'A marvellous decorative architectural plant'
SUFFOLK HERBS

Bud

The cardoon bud starts life the size of a gooseberry and grows quickly, reaching up to 13cm (5in) across just before it flowers.

Bloom

Guaranteed to catch your eye, the large flowerheads of the cardoon are carried on top of stout, woolly stems above the foliage, appearing from early summer onwards.

Foliage

Cardoons are grown for their outstanding foliage as much as for their flowers. The jagged leaves, sometimes up to 50cm (20in) long, arch out backwards from the stem, providing a breathtaking spectacle as they increase in size.

Height to 2.5m (8ft)
Spread to 1.5m (5ft)

Cultivation

Native to the Mediterranean, cardoons need a sheltered, sunny spot to thrive. Position them in fertile, well-drained soil, and they will reward you by growing swiftly. The plant is fully hardy, but where temperatures fall below −15°C (5°F), protect the overwintering root with a dry mulch.

Propagation

Growing from seed is a slow process, so it is best to propagate by division in late spring. Root cuttings can be taken in winter.

Pests and diseases

The cardoon is susceptible to grey mould (botrytis), slugs and aphids.

Associations

Cardoons look great with or without a supporting cast. They form a good backdrop to a multitude of plants – in spring, late-flowering white or purple tulips can be a good combination with the silver-grey foliage.

Seed

The seedheads of the cardoon are almost as striking as the flowers. Tough, spiky bracts contrast with soft, fluffy cream-coloured seeds that eventually disintegrate, leaving the spiky head to add interest to the winter garden.

Bronze fennel

Foeniculum vulgare 'Purpureum'

Bronze fennel is truly a plant for all the senses. Pleasing to the eye with its frothy clouds of burnished foliage, it is also very tactile, its soft feathery leaves inviting you to touch. Smell and taste are important too; crushed between your fingers, the leaves release their aromatic scent and both leaves and seed have a strong aniseed flavour. A versatile and easy plant that fits in with almost any planting scheme, fennel is a swift grower given the right conditions – a sunny space and well-drained soil – and it makes a useful filler for the herbaceous border with its bushy habit and tall stature. Although the foliage is the winning feature of this plant (and forms the derivative of its name, from the Latin *foenum* meaning hay) the flowers have their own merits. The large, flat umbels of rich yellow flowers are ejected upwards on long stems in midsummer, adding even more height.

'So gladiators fierce and rude, mingled it with their daily food'
HENRY WADSWORTH LONGFELLOW

Fennel has long been used for culinary and medicinal purposes. The Greeks used it as a slimming aid – it is said to suppress the appetite – while the Romans valued it as a culinary herb, using its leaf, root and seeds in stews and salads, and baking it in bread and cakes. Warriors would eat it to keep fit and healthy during battle, while Roman ladies took it to prevent obesity. In America, the seeds became known as the 'meeting seeds' because they were taken to church to drive away hunger pangs during long services. In English folklore, fennel was attributed with magical properties, hung over the door to keep fire away and to ward off evil spirits. Today, both seed and leaf are used in cooking, as a flavouring for fish and meat, and to make a tea which will aid digestion. You will often find a bowl of fennel seeds in an Indian restaurant to eat after the meal.

Bud

The graceful buds of bronze fennel appear in mid summer on slender branching stems.

Bloom

Like yellow cow parsley,
the flowerheads of
bronze fennel are held
above the feathery foliage
in flat umbels, and can
measure up to 10cm (4in)
across. If you look
closely you can see that
each umbel consists
of hundreds of tiny,
delicate flowers.

Foliage

Silky soft to the touch, the foliage is the reason to grow bronze fennel. The young growth, emerging from a long, furled 'ear' is especially dark and burnished, becoming greener with age. The leaves are very finely cut, and grow up to 30cm (12in) long. Use the leaves, chopped, as an accompaniment for fish or meat.

Height 1.8m (6ft)
Spread 45cm (18in)

Cultivation

Bronze fennel needs remarkably little attention other than a sunny aspect and a fertile, well-drained soil. Some of the flowerheads can be cut in late summer and the seed saved for the following year. Fennel is fully hardy, although young growth may be damaged by severe frost.

Propagation

Sow seed in spring *in situ*, or in a cold frame at 13–18°C (55–65°F).

Pests and diseases

When the plants are very young, root rot may occur if they are over-watered. Infestations of greenfly are sometimes known. This can be treated with horticultural soap.

Associations

The frothy bronze foliage looks good with many other plants, contrasting with most foliage shapes. For a hazy effect, plant with Russian sage (*perovskia*). Christopher Lloyd suggests combining it with yellow tulips.

Seed

Sparce and spiky, the seedheads of bronze fennel can provide interest in the autumn border. They bear tiny aromatic seeds that can be used for sauces and flavourings. Here, the seeds have long gone, leaving skeletons which remain throughout the winter. The seedheads can be dried for arrangements by hanging them upside-down.

Sea holly

Eryngium bourgatii

Bud

Eryngium bourgatii is not a large plant, rarely growing to more than 60cm (24in) high. But from early spring, when the first fresh lime-green buds emerge, the plant is already a serious competitor for visual interest in the border.

'The roots... are exceeding good to be given unto old and aged people'
JOHN GERARD

Like a handsome stranger, *Eryngium bourgatii* is a plant to be admired from afar. With needle-sharp leaves and spiny flowerheads, it has its own form of armour that keeps the predators away. A member of the carrot family *(Apeaceae)* – not the thistle family as you might expect – it is one of 30 or so species of eryngium originating from Europe, all of which are known by the common name, sea holly. This name relates specifically to the seaside-dwelling *E. maritimum* which grows wild in some parts of Britain and elsewhere in Europe, and it is this form that was used in the past as a medicinal herb. In Anglo-Saxon times, the aromatic root was used as an aphrodisiac, while in an Irish herbal of 1753, the writer states that the herb 'provokes urination and menstruation and encourages flatulence'. From 1600 to 1900 the root of the plant was used to make restorative lozenges and sweetmeats, known as 'eryngoes'.

In the garden, sea holly is grown for its strong, architectural shapes, but there is also a good range of colour among the different species. *E. bourgatii* is one of the most attractive, with purple-blue stems and silver-veined leaves, reaching its peak in midsummer with wonderful spiky flowers exploding outwards in a mass of steely blue. In autumn, this intense colour starts to fade, but the stems and flowerheads provide useful structure when other plants are dying back. Sea holly contrasts well with softer tones and textures. In her famous modern-day gravel garden, Beth Chatto combines *Eryngium bourgatii* with the yellow saucer-like flowers of *Achillea* 'Moonshine', while in Gertrude Jekyll's Grey Walk at Hestercombe in Somerset, sea holly is mixed with plants of a similar colour in a watercolour-wash of hazy blue.

Bloom

The flowerhead of
Eryngium bourgatii is a
real crown of thorns.
Delicately tinged with the
plant's trademark
violet-blue, the outer
circle of spiky bracts,
typically about 5cm (2in)
long, surrounds a central
domed teasel-like
inflorescence of the same
colour. On a mature plant
in midsummer, there can
be dozens of flowers
radiating outwards on
wiry stems.

Foliage

If the flowers of Eryngium bourgatii *didn't exist, the plant would still be worth growing for its splendid foliage. Veined with silver and white, the narrow, spiky leaves grow to 10cm (4in) long, and form neat rosettes around the stems – a perfect foil for the spiky flowers.*

Height to 45cm (18in)
Spread 30cm (12in)

Cultivation
Native to the Pyrenees, *Eryngium bourgatii* is a tough plant that will withstand all but the driest conditions. It thrives in open, sunny gardens in any well-drained soil, and tolerates poor soil remarkably well. It can also be grown through gravel. The plant is fully hardy and will tolerate frosts of up to –10ºC (14°F)

Propagation
Sea holly can be grown from seed collected in late summer or autumn. Plant seed straight away in pots and keep in a cold frame or greenhouse over winter. Plants can also be divided in spring, although they are slow to re-establish.

Pests and diseases
Sea holly is prone to root rot if exposed to prolonged damp conditions, so should be planted in well-drained soil.

Associations
Sea holly can provide contrast in colour and shape with plants such as achillea, Californian poppy or santolina, or it can be planted to blend in with the colour scheme in a border of lavenders, for example. It also looks good with other architectural plants such as phormiums or echinops. And why not try planting more than one species of eryngium? *Eryngium giganteum* is taller and more silvery, while *E.* x *oliverianum* has more pronounced cones to its flowerheads, and darker green leaves.

Seed

When other plants are dying back in the autumn, Eryngium bourgatii *still holds its own. Although its colour fades into tones of tawny brown, the structure of the plant remains intact, the starry seedheads providing architectural interest well into winter.*

Hellebore

Helleborus x hybridus

Bud

Emerging in late winter or early spring, the hellebore bud is borne on stout, hollow stems that grow up to 40cm (16in) high.

If you're a year-round gardener you'll already have discovered the unique qualities of the hellebore. While most perennials sleep soundly during the winter, the warm-blooded hellebore is awake, bursting into sumptuous flower even when the snow is lying thick on the ground. An evergreen perennial with bold, dark green leaves and pastel flowers, *Helleborus* x *hybridus* is one of the most popular and easy-going of the 15 different groups in the genus, happy in either sun or shade. Its family tree, however, is confusing. The plant has hybridized freely over the years with the result that it flowers in many different colours, from pure white to dusky plum – but if anything, this adds to its charm rather than detracts.

'Hellebores are an addiction'
CHRISTOPHER LLOYD

The pretty, cup-like flowers, angled slightly downwards in a demure fashion, belie the true nature of the hellebore, which is in fact highly toxic – a characteristic that is reflected in the name, a combination of the Greek *helein*, to kill, and *bora*, food. The leaves and roots of *Helleborus niger* (the white Christmas rose) were used by Hippocrates as far back as 2,200 years ago as a drug, and Pliny referred to it as a purgative, as a cure for lunacy and as a rat poison. According to one legend, it was favoured by witches, who used it in their evil charms. Even the collecting of hellebores was considered dangerous: Pliny advised reciting spells or prayers while lifting the root, and to look east and west to make sure eagles weren't watching. He also warned 'not to give hellebore to aged people or children, to persons of… a delicate or tender constitution'. Later, in the seventeenth century, John Gerard recommended a dose of hellebore for those 'molested by melancholy'. Nowadays it is regarded as too poisonous to use in any medicine, but its stature as a garden plant has never been higher.

Bloom

The graceful flowers of the hellebore face bravely outwards managing to withstand the winter weather. Up to 8cm (3in) across, the flowers are often attractively freckled on the insides, with numerous golden yellow stamens adding even more charm. After eight to ten weeks the colour starts to fade, but the blooms will not disintegrate for many months.

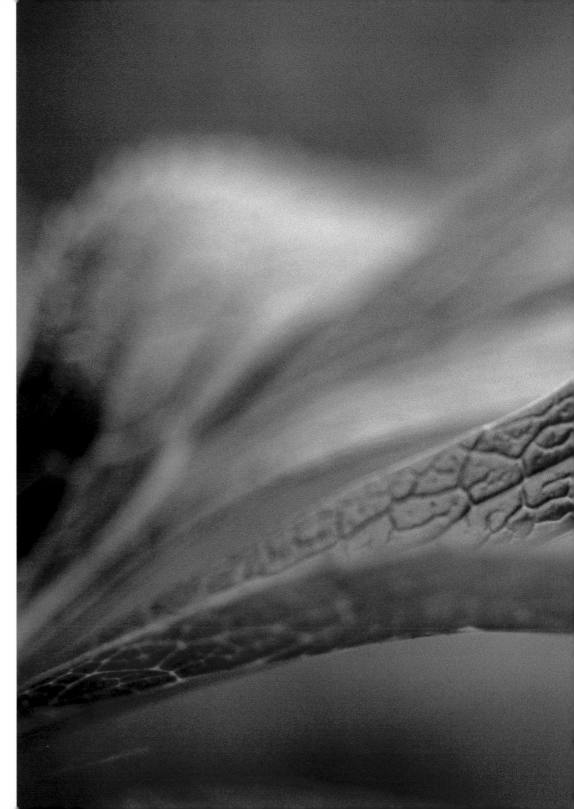

Foliage

Forming a good strong base for the blooms, the large, dark green leaves of the hellebore are leathery in texture and robust enough to survive low temperatures. The foliage increases throughout the growing season, and once the flowers set seed it takes over, making sure the plant remains a focal point throughout the summer months.

Height 45cm (18in)
Spread 45cm (18in)

Cultivation

Hellebores will grow in sun or shade, although they perform best in semi-shade, perhaps at the edge of woodland or in a shrub border. Grow in deep, rich soil with a top-dressing of compost or well-rotted manure. They like moist conditions but will not survive if waterlogged, so ensure the soil is well drained.

Propagation

Hellebores can be grown from seed, although it will take two to three years for them to flower. Sow seed in a cold frame as soon as ripe, or divide species or named cultivars after flowering.

Pests and diseases

The young leaves can be susceptible to snails, aphids, leaf spot and black spot.

Associations

Grow the hellebore with a range of early spring bulbs such as snowdrops, chionodoxas or an early yellow daffodil. Hellebores also look good against a shrubby backdrop – use shrubs with pale-coloured foliage to show up dark-flowered forms and vice versa.

Seed

After six to eight weeks, the colour of the hellebore blooms begins to fade and the stamens disintegrate. The stigma develop into seed pods, pale green at first, maturing to husky brown as the seeds ripen.

Coneflower

Echinacea purpurea

Bud

The coneflower bud appears in early summer pushing purposefully up through the surrounding foliage – one bud per stem so there is no competition. Each bud is surrounded protectively by stiff, pointed scales (see page 8) which will eventually be obscured as the petals emerge (as shown here).

Tall, statuesque and stunningly beautiful, the coneflower is the supermodel of perennials. On top of long, willowy stems, its richly coloured daisy-like flowers sport elegant petals that droop in a kind of sultry pout around a central rusty-red 'cone' of prickles. Flowering from midsummer until early autumn, it is currently high in the fashion stakes as a garden plant, mixing comfortably in the herbaceous border with a medley of other late-flowering perennials or ornamental grasses. It looks best planted in large drifts, mimicking its natural occurrence in the prairies of North America. Think of its natural habitat when positioning in the garden – a well-drained, open site is best for this sunworshipper, and if it is given the right conditions it will reward you by growing tall and strong with large, luscious blooms. When the petals drop in autumn, the central prickly cone remains intact to leave interesting-looking lollipops that dry to a chocolaty brown – it is this cone that gives the plant its name, from the Greek *echinos*, meaning hedgehog. There are several cultivars to try: 'Magnus' is the giant of the species, with magenta blooms up to 18cm (7¼in) in diameter, while 'White Lustre' or the unusual 'Green Edge' offer paler accents.

'The large cones serve as landing platforms for bees and butterflies'
ANTHONY BROOKS

Echinacea is a plant that may be more familiar to some people in a rather different context, for it is one of the world's most important medicinal herbs, used to stimulate the immune system and taken in the form of tablets and tinctures to ward off common germs and viruses. It was also employed by the native Americans, who cultivated the plant for its root, using it to treat wounds and as an antidote to insect and rattlesnake bites – hence the common names 'rattlesnake weed' and 'scurvy root'.

Bloom

The flowers of Echinacea purpurea, *up to 15cm (6in) in diameter, are show-offs in the summer border. Brightly coloured and sometimes sweetly scented, their magenta petals and large rusty brown cones create an interesting colour combination that makes you look twice. Growing on stems of up to 1.5m (5 ft) in height, they rise head and shoulders above many other plants. Grow them en masse for a spectacular display.*

Foliage

The coneflower is a leafy plant with dark green, bristly foliage to complement the flowers. The basal leaves can grow up to 15cm (6in) long, while higher up, smaller leaves branch from the hairy, sometimes red-tinted stem.

Height up to 1.5m (5ft)
Spread 45cm (18in)

Cultivation
The coneflower is fully hardy and is easy to cultivate if given the right conditions. Grow in deep, well-drained, humus-rich soil in full sun (although it will tolerate some shade). Cut back the stems as the blooms begin to fade to encourage further flowering.

Propagation
Coneflowers are easily raised from seed, which should be sown in spring. Sow on to damp compost and tamp down, but don't cover the seed as darkness will reduce the chance of germination. They can also be propagated by division, in spring or autumn, but too much disturbance can be detrimental.

Pests and diseases
Coneflowers are remarkably free from pests and diseases.

Associations
Plant with other late-flowering perennials like Japanese anemones, sidalceas, sedums, Michaelmas daisies or the coneflower's yellow cousins, rudbeckias. It also looks striking amongst clumps of ornamental grasses such as miscanthus, pennisetum and panicums.

Seed

When the petals disappear in autumn, the conical centres of the coneflower are left to create their own drama. Often used by flower arrangers, the spiky seedheads can also be left in the border to mature gracefully from tawny brown to almost black as the winter sets in.

Peony (Molly the witch)

Paeonia mlokosewitschii

Bud

The pale, fat, round buds of Peony Molly the witch appear on purple-tinged stems in late spring.

Named after Paeon, physician to the Greek gods, the peony is one of the most well-loved herbaceous perennials in the garden, its showy flowers providing a short-lived but spectacular display each spring. Paeon was said to be the first to discover the plant's medicinal properties, and thereafter until the sixteenth century the root was used to treat lunacy, epilepsy, nightmares and convulsions. It was also said to drive away storms and evil spirits.

'Few plants have such direct appeal'
GRAHAM STUART THOMAS

There are more than 30 species in the genus, divided into two types – the herbaceous perennials and the shrubby 'tree peonies' – and of the herbaceous peonies, *Paeonia mlokosewitschii* is possibly the most distinguished. The uncrowned queen of the border, it is affectionately known as Molly the witch due to its unpronounceable name, and was introduced into Western cultivation in 1900, having been discovered by its namesake Ludwik Mlokosiewicz, a naturalist and forester from the Caucasus.

Truly a plant for all seasons, Molly the witch isn't only admired for its beguiling lemon-yellow flowers, and should be given pride of place in a border. One of the earliest peonies to appear in spring, it begins the year with a burst of colour, sending up deep red shoots through the soil that gradually unfold into reddish-brown leaves. By the time the flowers appear in late spring, the foliage has turned blue-green, sometimes retaining a red tinge around the edge of each leaf; then after flowering it changes yet again, taking on a deep purple hue. The large, abundant flowers are undoubtedly the highlight of the year, dotted almost symmetrically over the neat mound of foliage – but they can be short-lived, particularly in wet or windy weather. This is made up for by the large, colourful seedheads, however, whose berries make a good winter meal for the birds.

Bloom

The appearance of the bowl-shaped lemon-yellow flowers of Peony Molly the witch is one of the highlights of the year. With pleasingly uniform petals surrounding a central disk of golden stamens, the blooms can grow to 12cm (5in) across. Sadly, the flowers last only two or three weeks.

Foliage

The chameleon-like foliage of Peony Molly the witch is part of this peony's huge charm. Deep red when they first emerge, the ovate leaves mature to a blue grey, sometimes tinged with red. Then in autumn they change to purple.

Seed

More fruit than seed, the large seed capsules of Peony Molly the witch split to reveal glossy bluish-black berries that stand out against the red background of the pod.

Height 90cm (36in)
Spread 90cm (36in)

Cultivation
Peony Molly the witch thrives in deep, fertile and well-drained soil in full sun. Little attention is needed when established, but it is best not to move or disturb the plant as this may stop it from flowering.

Propagation
Sow seed in containers in autumn or winter, but be prepared for a long wait, as it can take two or three years to germinate. Root cuttings can be taken in winter.

Pests and diseases
Susceptible to viruses, eelworms and honey fungus. Peony wilt may destroy shoots and buds.

Associations
The yellow blooms of Peony Molly the witch look especially good with blue. Try it next to a sky-blue ceanothus, or underplanted with bluebells.

Pasque flower

Pulsatilla vulgaris

Bud

The downy buds of the Pasque flower appear around Easter time each year on stems that rise above the foliage.

Small, but perfectly formed, the Pasque flower stands for all that is new and joyous about spring. Defying cold weather and frozen soil, its ferny shoots push up through the ground in early spring, while the flowers appear at Easter time – hence the name, derived from the word 'paschal'. One of about 30 species of pulsatilla, *P. vulgaris* is naturalized in many parts of Europe. In Britain, it remains in only a few rare remaining pockets of untouched chalk or lime grassland. As a garden plant, however, it is popular, grown as much for its soft, silvery seedheads as for its simple but eye-catching flowers. Every part of the plant is soft to the touch – the stems are covered with downy hair, the petals have the texture of rich velvet, while the seedheads, magical when they catch the light or glisten in the early morning dew, are like the finest silk.

'Flowers of great beauty'
JOHN GERARD

A small, mound-forming plant, the Pasque flower is best suited to a rock garden or alpine garden, with other low-growing plants, but it can also look effective at the front of a border. At Vita Sackville-West's famous garden at Sissinghurst in Kent it is grown in the herb garden, where in summer its seedheads are flanked by feverfew, artemisia, thyme and sage. Used at one time to make a green dye for Easter eggs, the plant has few other practical uses, but its beauty has captivated plant-lovers for hundreds of years. John Gerard referred to the plant as the 'Passe Floure', or 'Bastard Anemone', while William Robinson talks about it as 'one of the plants more beautiful in a wild state than in a garden'. Present-day writer and gardener Mirabel Osler sums up the thrill of the first sight of the Pasque flower in spring: 'I could hardly believe that such an exquisite thing could emerge when the earth was still cold'.

Bloom

The flowers of the Pasque flower are usually mauve or purple, although white and red forms also exist. Growing up to 9cm (3½in) across, the flowers are bell-shaped and nodding, each consisting of six soft petals surrounding a central boss of bright yellow stamens.

Foliage

Verdant green and silky soft to the touch, the foliage of the Pasque flower is in keeping with the velvety textures of the rest of the plant. The leaves, which can grow up to 20cm (8in) long, are finely divided and fern-like, and covered in fine hairs when young. The foliage remains long after the seedheads have disappeared in summer.

Height 25cm (10in)
Spread 20cm (8in)

Seed

Like a shock of wispy hair, the seedheads of the Pasque flower are feathery and plume-like, catching the light to create a silvery effect. Although it is low-growing in bloom, after flowering the stems elongate considerably to carry the spherical seedheads (see also pages 90–91).

Cultivation

Grow the Pasque flower in full sun, in fertile, very well-drained soil, with an added dressing of grit if necessary. Do not allow it to become waterlogged. The plants do not like root disturbance, and can sometimes be difficult to establish, so plant when small and leave undisturbed. The plant is fully hardy, indeed it seems to thrive in colder conditions.

Propagation

The plant grows easily from seed, or can be propagated by root cuttings taken in winter. Sow seed in pots as soon as ripe, and keep in an open cold frame.

Pests and diseases

Young growth may be attacked by slugs and snails.

Associations

A good plant for a rock garden, Pasque flowers look great with other spring bloomers such as gentians, chionodoxas and pulmonarias. In summer, their seedheads are complemented by lavender, thyme and other herbs.

Bugbane

Cimicifuga simplex 'Brunette'

Bud

The buds of Cimicifuga *simplex* 'Brunette' *appear on long, often purple-tinged stems at the end of summer.*

Bugbane is one of those tall, late-flowering perennials that have become rather fashionable in recent years, used widely in the planting schemes favoured by European garden designers such Dutchman Piet Oudolf. Christopher Lloyd calls it a 'see-through plant', but that doesn't mean it is insignificant. With arching wands of creamy flowers that sway gracefully on long stems, this is a sociable plant rather than a loner, acting as a frame through which other plants can be woven and mixing happily with other late-flowering perennials and grasses. *Cimicifuga simplex* 'Brunette' is one of the loveliest cultivars, standing out from the crowd with its superb dark purple foliage and delicate white, honey-scented flowers, sometimes tinged with a hint of pink. Part of the buttercup *(Ranunculacae)* family, *C. simplex* is one of 18 species in the genus, originating from Russia, Asia and North America. It is reliably the last in the genus to flower, making it a useful plant for the autumn garden, with the added bonus that once the flowers have gone, the brown, bobbly, bottlebrush seedheads last well into winter.

'An extraordinary perennial'
DAN HINKLEY

Both botanical and common names derive from the Latin *cimex* (bug) and *fugo* (to put to flight), and relate to the sister species *Cimicifuga foetidus*, a foul-smelling plant which at the time when the botanist Linnaeus named the plant in 1750, was ground into a powder and stuffed into mattresses and pillows to drive away bugs. A number of other species are used in herbal medicine, particularly *C. racemosa*. Also known as black cohosh or squaw root, the root of this plant has oestrogenic properties, and has been used for centuries to treat gynaecological problems. It is also used for inflammatory disorders like arthritis, and as a sedative to treat conditions such as high blood pressure and asthma.

Bloom

*The fluffy, pinky-white
bugbane flowers appear
in late summer on robust,
arching stems. Crowded
together in tapering,
bottlebrush-like racemes,
up to 30cm (12in) long,
the tiny star-like flowers
are often sweetly
scented, making them
especially attractive to
bees and butterflies.*

Foliage

Like many other plants in the buttercup family, bugbane leaves break through the soil in tight, ruffled clusters that are most pleasing to the eye. The dark, burnished purple of the leaves distinguishes 'Brunette' from other forms.

Height 2m (6ft)
Spread 60cm (24in)

Cultivation

Grow bugbane in moist, preferably acidic soil, with plenty of organic matter incorporated. It prefers a cool situation in partial shade and, despite its height, needs no support.

Propagation

Growing cimicifugas from seed can be a long process, because they need long periods of frost and low temperatures to germinate. An easier way to propagate is to divide mature clumps in spring.

Pests and diseases

Bugbane is relatively untroubled by pests or disease.

Associations

Cimicifuga simplex 'Brunette' looks effective planted with drifts of other late-flowering perennials such as achilleas and monardas. Piet Oudolf recommends planting it with a dark astrantia such as 'Claret', or to grow up above grasses such as miscanthus and *Stipa calamagrostis*.

Seed

Bugbane sets seed rapidly and copiously. The small white flowers fall cleanly and quickly, leaving attractive, greeny purple seedheads that turn golden brown in the winter.

Golden groundsel

Ligularia dentata 'Desdemona'

Bud

Cradled by two curled leaves, the fat, round buds of 'Desdemona' appear in clusters, soon to explode into fiery colour as the flowers come out.

'She that was ever fair and never proud'
SHAKESPEARE'S *Othello*

Unlike the Shakespearean heroine, who perished at the hands of Othello, this Desdemona is a winner. Bold, striking and robust, with its large leaves and bright orange daisy-like flowers, *Ligularia dentata* 'Desdemona' packs the punches from all sides. Even before the flowers appear in midsummer, the leaves create their own drama with their unusual purple-red undersides, looking almost like stained glass with the sun shining through them. The show continues equally effectively later in the season when dark, round buds appear on branching stems above the leaves, finally exploding into clusters of orange flowers – the perfect supporting role to the foliage's lead. The flowers are long-lived, lasting well into autumn, and develop into soft, fluffy seedheads which, like dandelions, are dispersed by the wind. Originating from China, *Ligularia dentata* was first introduced into Western cultivation around the beginning of the twentieth century by Ernest Wilson. 'Desdemona' appeared in 1940, and comes highly recommended as one of only two ligularias to win a Royal Horticultural Society Award of Garden Merit.

The best stage-set for this showy plant is a moist or even boggy area with plenty of space, offering a mixture of sun and shade – perhaps near a pond or on the edge of woodland. It will survive in full sun, but the leaves tend to wilt if the sun is too strong, so a constant supply of water is even more important. Given the right conditions, it will form large clumps, creating good ground cover with its rhubarb-like leaves and looking most spectacular in large drifts. Ligularias can be vulnerable to attack by slugs and snails in spring, but a strong argument for cultivating this plant in spite of this are the flowers, which are especially attractive to butterflies, a bonus for a wildlife-friendly garden.

Bloom

Ideal for brightening up a dull corner of the garden, the brightly coloured daisy-like flowers of 'Desdemona' unfurl in the sun. Gathered in clusters on branching, red-stalked stems, they can grow up to 10cm (4in) across, appearing in midsummer and lasting well into autumn.

Foliage

*The foliage of
'Desdemona' is its* pièce
de résistance. *Up to
30cm (12in) long, the
large, kidney-shaped
leaves are metallic
grey-green on top and
purple-red on the
undersides, and look
particularly fine with the
sun shining through them.*

Height 1–1.2m (3ft 3in–4ft)
Spread 0.75–1m (2½–3ft)

Cultivation
Grow in deep, moist, fertile soil, in dappled shade, preferably by a pond or stream, or near woodland. The soil must not be left to dry out otherwise the plant will wilt. If given plenty of space, it will spread rapidly to give excellent ground cover. The plant is fully hardy.

Propagation
Sow seed in containers in autumn or spring, or divide established plants in spring or after flowering.

Pests and diseases
Slugs and snails may damage the foliage, especially the young leaves in spring.

Associations
Christopher Lloyd suggests making the most of the spring foliage by planting it with a good red tulip such as 'Halco'. You could also try mixing it with another moisture-lover, *Cimicifuga racemosa*, whose white bottle-brush spires will contrast dramatically with the orange flowers in late summer.

Seed

Designed to be dispersed by the wind, the fluffy brown seedheads of 'Desdemona' can look effective in the autumn garden, and are also fairly slow to disintegrate. When the seeds have gone, a small round globe is all that remains, likened by a seventeenth-century herbalist to a 'balde-headed man'.

Sources

Plants, seeds and national collection holders

UK

Bernwode Plants
Kingswood Lane,
Ludgershall,
Aylesbury,
Buckinghamshire HP18 9RB
tel: 01844 237415
www.bernwodeplants.co.uk

Beth Chatto Nursery & Gardens
Elmstead Market,
Colchester,
Essex CO7 7DB
tel: 01206 822007
www.bethchatto.co.uk

Cotswold Garden Flowers
Sands Lane,
Badsey,
Evesham,
Worcestershire WR11 5EZ
tel: 01386 833849
Mail order: 01386 422829
www.cgf.net

Crûg Farm Plants
Griffiths Crossing,
Caernarfon,
Gwynedd LL55 1TU
tel: 01248 670232
www.curg-farm.demon.co.uk
No mail order

Four Seasons Nursery
Forncett St Mary,
Norwich NR16 1JT
tel: 01508 488344
www.fsperennials.co.uk
Mail order only

Iden Croft Herbs
Frittenden Road,
Staplehurst,
Kent TN12 0DH
tel: 01580 891432
www.herbs-uk.com

R D Plants
Homelea Farm,
Chard Road,
Tytherleigh,
Axminster,
Devon EX13 7BG
tel: 01460 220206
(8.30-9.30am)
No mail order

Rushfields of Ledbury
Ross Road,
Ledbury,
Herefordshire HR8 2LP
tel: 01531 632004
www.rushfieldsofledbury.co.uk
No mail order

Stillingfleet Lodge Nurseries
Stillingfleet,
York YO19 6HP
tel: 01904 728506

Woottens Plants
Blackheath,
Wenhaston,
Halesworth,
Suffolk IP19 9HD
tel: 01502 478258

USA & CANADA
A&D Peony & Perennial
Nursery
6808 180th SE,
Snohomish,
WA 98296
tel: 001 360 668 9690
www.speciality-nurseries.com

Blanchette Gardens
267 Rutland St.,
Carlisle,
MA 01741
tel: 001 978 369 2962
www.blanchettegardens.com

The Herb Cottage
Rt 2 Box 90,
Hallettsville,
TX 77964
tel: 001 409 562 2153

Heronswood Nursery Ltd
7530 NE 288th St.,
Kingston,
WA 98346
tel: 001 360 297 4172
www.heronswood.com

Lazy S's Farm Nursery
2360 Spotswood Trail,
Barboursville,
VA 22923
tel: 001 540 832 2334

Madrona Nursery
815 38th Ave.,
Seattle,
WA 98122
tel: 001 206 323 8325

Specialty Perennials
481 Reflection Rd.,
Apple Valley,
MN 55124
tel: 001 612 432 8673

The Perennial Gardens Inc.
13139 224th St.,
Maple Ridge,
BC V4R 2P6
Canada
tel: 001 604 467 4218
www.perennialgardener.com

National Collections, UK
These are collections of plants of a single genus where different species and cultivars can be seen together and compared. Please telephone in advance to view a collection.

Aquilegia
Mr J. Drake
Hardwicke House,
Fenditton,
Cambridge CB5 8TF
tel: 01223 292 246

Cimicifuga
Mr C. Sanders
Bridgemere Nurseries,
Bridgemere,
Nr Nantwich,
Cheshire CW5 7QB
tel: 01270 521100

Cynara and Foeniculum
Beth Chatto Gardens
Elmstead Market,
Colchester,
Essex CO7 7DB
tel: 01206 822007

Echinacea
Mr A. Brooks
Elton Hall,
Elton,
Nr Ludlow,
Herefordshire
tel: 01568 770218

Eryngium
Mr J. Lamont
Myerscough College,
Myerscough Hall,
Bilsborrow,
Preston,
Lancs PR3 0RY
tel: 01995 640611

Helleborus
Mr K. Mehdi
Hadlow College,
Hadlow,
Tonbridge,
Kent TN11 0AL
tel: 01732 850551

Ligularia
Mrs A. Benson
Fell Yeat,
Casterton,
Cumbria LA6 2JW
tel: 01524 271340

Paeonia
Mr R. Mitchell
Kingscroft,
Elie,
Fife KY9 1BY
tel: 01333 330642

Pulsatilla
Sissinghurst Castle Garden
Sissinghurst,
Cranbrook,
Kent TN17 2AB
tel: 01580 710701

Acknowledgements

I would like to dedicate this book to my friend and neighbour June Rogers for all her help and inspiration in this project, and for caring for my garden in my absence.

Also many thanks to Leslie Forbes, who started the process of turning my idea into a reality; and to Caz and Clare whose design and words have given it life, with much help from Muna and all the crew at Conran. Last, but not least, love and thanks to my partner Shaun, for all his encouragement and input.

Carol Sharp
www.carolsharp.co.uk

Thanks to the following sources for use of quotes: Page 11: Helen Dillon on Gardening by Helen Dillon, published by Town House Publishing, 1998. Page 19: Suffolk Herbs Catalogue, 2000. Page 27: Byerly's food website, www.byerlys.com. Page 35: Gerard's Herball, Dover, 1975. Page 43: Christopher Lloyd's Garden Flowers by Christopher Lloyd, published by Cassell & Co, 2000. Page 51: article by Anthony Brookes in Gardens Illustrated Magazine, 1999. Page 59: Perennial Garden Plants by Graham Stuart Thomas, published by J.M. Dent, 1976. Page 67: Gerard's Herball, Dover, 1975. Page 75, Dan Hinkley in the Seattle Times.

Every effort has been made to trace the copyright holders and we apologise in advance for any unintentional omissions and would be pleased to insert the appropriate acknowledgement in any subsequent publication.